Learning a New Routine

Reading the Sermon on the Mount a little bit at a time (Matthew 5:1-7:29)

Jon Swanson

Copyright © 2012 by Jon C Swanson

Preface to paperback edition copyright © 2023 by Jon C Swanson

All rights reserved

Scripture taken from the HOLY BIBLE, NEW INTERNATIONAL VERSION®. Copyright © 1973, 1978, 1984 Biblica. Used by permission of Zondervan. All rights reserved.

The "NIV" and "New International Version" trademarks are registered in the United States Patent and Trademark Office by Biblica. Use of either trademark requires the permission of Biblica.

Cover photo: Jon Swanson

Cover design: Paul Merrill

No portion of this book may be reproduced in any form without written permission from the publisher or author, except as permitted by U.S. copyright law.

Contents

Preface to Paperback Edition VI
Introduction VII
1. What counts as poor in spirit? (Matthew 5:1-2) 1
2. The stripped-down truth (Matthew 5:1-10) 3
3. But following won't be easy (Matthew 5:11-12) 5
4. Be something useful (Matthew 5:13-16) 7
5. Not good enough (Matthew 5:20) 9
6. You have heard it said (Matthew 5:21) 11
7. I'm sorry you are mad at me (Matthew 5:23-24) 13
8. Lust is an action (Matthew 5:27-30) 15
9. But you said. . . (Matthew 5:33-37) 17
10. You caught me skipping (Matthew 5:31-32) 19
11. So, what about divorce? (Matthew 5:31-32) 21
12. Someone in your life is going to go too far (Matthew 5:38-42) 23
13. Be like God (Matthew 5:43-48) 25
14. Like the hypocrites do (Matthew 6:1-18) 27
15. "I love to hear you pray" (Matthew 6:5-6) 29

16.	So why do we have to ask? (Matthew 6:7-8)	31
	The Lord's Prayer: a preface (Matthew 6:9-13)	33
17.	Lord's Prayer: Our Father in heaven (Matthew 6:9)	34
18.	Lord's Prayer: We pray that your name will always be kept holy (6:9)	36
19.	Lord's Prayer: Your kingdom (Matthew 6:10)	38
20.	Lord's Prayer: Enough for today (Matthew 6:11)	40
21.	Lord's Prayer: That is really hard (Matthew 6:11)	42
22.	Lord's Prayer: Please take care of me (Matthew 6:12-13)	44
23.	Fasting (Matthew 6:16-18)	46
24.	Relationship rewards (Matthew 6:20)	49
25.	Birds and flowers (Matthew 6:25-34)	51
26.	Today has enough trouble (Matthew 6:34)	53
27.	The window or the mirror (Matthew 7:1-2)	55
28.	A sense of humor (Matthew 7)	57
29.	On hogs and dogs (Matthew 7:6)	59
30.	Waiting is hard (Matthew 7:7-12)	61
31.	Wanna do something about it? (Matthew 7:12)	64
32.	Gates (Matthew 7:13-14)	66
33.	Aftermath (Matthew 7:15-23)	68
34.	Just one thing (Matthew 7:24)	70
35.	Sandstorm (Matthew 7:24-27)	72
36.	Routinely: a summary	74

Afterword 76

Preface to Paperback Edition

Learning a New Routine is based on posts I wrote during the first year of 300wordsaday.com.

I started that blog in 2009. After hearing a review of devotional books, and thinking "I could do that!", I wrote my way through the book of Matthew in 2009 a day at a time. Since then, I've written my way through a lot of life and the Bible. 300wordsaday.com is the daily devotional I said I could do and have been doing for 15 years as of December 2023.

In December 2012, I edited a series of Advent posts into my first ebook. Shortly after that, I put together the posts on the Sermon on the Mount, after polishing them for a few years, and published them as my second ebook.

Since then, I've written a lot about a lot of things. *Learning a New Routine* has been in the background, shaping my thinking, but not very accessible to people who like to hold a devotional book in their hands.

Recently, Nancy (my wife) read that ebook and said, "You should put this into a paperback."

It's likely that 2023 Jon would write these differently than 2009 Jon. But that's fine. 2023 Jon doesn't have the time to start over. I am leaving them as I wrote them, resisting the urge for explanatory footnotes.

I hope that you find these readings helpful.

Jon

October 2023 in Paradise, Michigan

Introduction

The way we live is a *routine*. When we get up, which path we take to work, what we do at work, how we spend our time when we have a choice, how we react when we don't have a choice. A routine is simply a set of thoughts and behaviors performed consistently. Gymnasts have routines. Actors have onstage routines, called scripts. And off-stage routines, called warmups. Parents create bed-time routines for their children.

We often find our routines to be routine, unexciting. We want to change them, to find excitement. And change is exciting. It throws everything off. But eventually, even the novelty becomes a routine and becomes *routine*.

Unless we find a template, a proven technique. Someone else's routine. I've done this often, looking at time management tools, attention management tools, life management tools. So have you. When we're done, we have built a collection of techniques. And we live our routine better, but sometimes we still wonder why we are doing this.

That's because routines are *how* to live. They need to have a *why*.

There are lots of whys available as well. And rather that look at all the options, I want to pick one and look at it. I want to invite you to spend some time with me looking at a sermon where Jesus describes learning a new routine.

This sermon answers a simple question: *What does the routine of the kingdom of heaven look like?* Before we can look at the sermon, to even understand the question, we need to look at Jesus.

When Jesus preached the Sermon on the Mount, his most familiar sermon, he was working close to home. In fact, most of his life happened in a country the size of Vermont or New Jersey.

He had been born in Bethlehem, a small town a few miles south of Jerusalem. He was taken to Egypt as a young child, fleeing religious persecution. After a couple years, he returned to Nazareth, a rural area about 65 miles north from Jerusalem geographically and a million miles culturally and socially.

We don't know much about what happened from the time his family returned to Nazareth and the time he started the preaching part of his life. Luke gives us the only glimpse. At age twelve, we find Jesus debating with and confounding the other rabbis and teachers of the law (Luke 2:39-52).

Around the age of thirty, he finds his relative, John. We know him as John the Baptist. He was called that because he lived near the Jordan River, and he baptized people. They repented from their sins, and he dipped them in the river. It symbolized the sins being washed away.

Jesus came one day to be baptized. John recognized him and wanted to change places, to be baptized by Jesus. After all, Jesus didn't have sins to repent from. Jesus refused. He wanted to live out the routine. He was baptized by John. There was a voice from heaven and a dove.

In addition to baptizing, John preached. The elevator version of John's message was simple: "Repent, for the kingdom of heaven is near." And then John got specific about what to repent of. His preaching got the attention of Herod, the son of the Herod the Great, the one who talked with the wise men. John spoke out about Herod's marriage. Herod locked him up.

When John was locked up, Jesus moved from Nazareth to Capernaum, a town at the top of the Sea of Galilee (a lake about twelve miles long and seven miles wide). It was a very short move. He started to preach, just like John: "Repent, for the kingdom of heaven is near."

People were excited about Jesus. He taught. He healed people. He preached. People walked for miles to hear him, to see him, to be touched by him. He was always compassionate, but he made it clear that his primary calling wasn't as a healer. One evening, early in his ministry, crowds showed up at the end of the day. He healed many, and then stopped for the night. Early in the morning, as the crowds began to wake up, his followers looked around for him. He was gone, off into the wilderness. When they found him, they were excited about the attention that his ministry was getting. He was going viral. He wouldn't go back. He left the sick people waiting. He went on to other towns.

His purpose was to proclaim the good news of the kingdom.

But what is this kingdom Jesus was talking about?

It was a question for the people living when Jesus lived. It's still a question that matters a lot to people who are interested, maybe, in following him. We want to know more about this kingdom. What are the rules, what are the boundaries, what are the expectations? And maybe, most importantly, what does it mean for me right now?

Jesus knew that people had these questions. He went up on a hillside one day. He sat on a rock. His followers, his fans, the curious, all gathered around. There were lots of people.

And he started to speak.

1

What counts as poor in spirit? (Matthew 5:1-2)

Jesus says "Blessed" nine times in the first few sentences of chapter 5. We look at this list, which is often called "The Beatitudes," and we try to figure out what Jesus meant. Actually, I think, we try to figure out how we can be part of the list.

We want to know because we like clear rules for success. Once we know the rules, then we can get whatever is in the formula. But I think that when Jesus gave this list of blessings, he wasn't creating a formula or a list. I think he was describing hope for people who are wrecked rather than creating formulas for people who think they're fine. The hard part of this teaching is that most of us don't want a new routine until we believe at our core that the old one and all its variations will still leave us poor in spirit.

For example, Jesus says that the poor in spirit will be blessed, that they will have the kingdom of heaven. So, wanting to have the kingdom of heaven, we ask what poor in spirit means. Does it relate to bank accounts, in which case it turns our usual expectations upside down (It sounds like an infomercial: "Don't have money in the bank? Don't worry your little soul. You have heaven!")? Does it mean being spiritually needy, in which case it applies to all of us even if we don't see it?

Here's what I think was happening on that hillside:

Jesus was walking with his followers near his hometown. He sat down on a stone on a hillside. His closest friends came and sat down with him. He looked around the circle. Others stood around the circle. He took time looking at their faces. He looked around at their hearts. And he knew what was in each.

The sky was clear, the Sea of Galilee was visible in the distance. He looked at one of the disciples, one that everyone knew was struggling. He had no interest in the view. His heart was aching. This man was despaired of ever measuring up spiritually in this group.

Jesus looked at the disciple and said, "Blessed are the poor in spirit." The disciple looked up, face drawn, eyes quizzical. "Theirs is the kingdom of heaven."

2

The stripped-down truth (Matthew 5:1-10)

Try a thought experiment with me. Strip away the two-syllable pronunciation of blessed ("bless-ed"). Take away the expectations associated with the "If this, then this" formula. Write the beatitudes out as a letter to a friend. It might sound something like this:

***

Dear friend.

You want to follow God.

But you feel like you have nothing to offer, like you are at a party where everyone else brings cool gifts, and you are still waiting for your last paycheck and so have nothing. You think about how you have done wrong and how often you have messed up, and it makes you want to cry. You watch other people push to the front with all the "right answers," and you stand back along the edges of the crowd, scuffing the dirt with your toes, uncertain. You want to live the right way so much you can taste it sometimes. You have a dull ache in your chest because you so want to be clean, finally, really clean.

Everyone tells you to slap those, um, *people* who mock you. You know you want to, but you just can't. You have this need to cut them slack. You try to stay clean. You try to do things for the right reasons. When you look in the mirror and have questions about your motives, you don't do whatever it is you are wondering about. (But doesn't everyone think that way?)

You can't stand watching people fight, and so you wade into the middle. But instead of just getting them to stop fighting, you start building bridges between them.

You do great stuff. You care deeply. And instead of thanking you, people pick on you. Mercilessly. Rudely. Maliciously.

You think all this is no big deal. You do it because it's right. You don't see the connection between any of this and following God.

But it *is* following God. Jesus says you are blessed. Jesus will comfort you and care for you and show you mercy and give you all of heaven.

3

But following won't be easy (Matthew 5:11-12)

Jesus is clear, though, right from the beginning paragraphs of this sermon, that the new routine will hurt. Not the pain of working muscles that haven't been used for a while, though that is certainly true. These sentences are more like the warnings of side effects we hear during every medicine commercial.

At the time Jesus spoke these words, they may have sounded unnecessarily somber. Within a year or two, and millennia later, these words aren't prophecy. They are the evening news. Around the world, Christ-followers are dying right now. At this moment.

I'll be more accurate. They are being killed right now. Because of Jesus. Because they decided, somewhere, somehow, to identify with Jesus, people are being killed and harassed and robbed and tortured and exiled.

Jesus was clear: being identified with Him is dangerous.

He said:

Blessed are you when people insult you, persecute you and falsely say all kinds of evil against you because of me. Rejoice and be glad, because great is your reward in heaven, for in the same way they persecuted the prophets who were before you.(Matthew 5:11-12)

And then, a couple years later, he was insulted, he was lied about, he was persecuted, and he was killed. He described in this sermon what happened to him, before it happened.

I find his words oddly comforting for a couple reasons.

First, he speaks historically about what only he would know. He says to rejoice because there will be a great reward in heaven. The prophets were persecuted and, he implies, they got a great reward in heaven. How would Jesus know that? He was there when they got the reward.

Second, he speaks predictively about what only he would know. He says to rejoice because there will be a great reward in heaven which, Paul says, happens to Jesus. According to Philippians 2:5-11, He (Jesus) willingly "became obedient to death." God then lifted him up.

But there is a condition in his blessing.

The persecution comes "because of me." It's a response to what Jesus said, not how we change it. Sometimes we decide what Jesus would like. We think that He would really like it if we told people to stay off the lawn he made, for example. We don't ask him, we just decide. We create our own routines. And then when people get mad, we think they're mad at him. They aren't. They are mad at us for deciding for him and for them what he is saying.

For this blessing, we have to speak as he speaks. And shut up when he does.

4

Be something useful (Matthew 5:13-16)

Jesus now talks about influence. He talks about salt and light.

Salt seasons. It preserves. It melts ice. It helps make homemade ice cream. It corrodes paint. It makes water undrinkable. Attached to your arm, it makes the same water support life. It is simple. It is natural. It is found in lots of locations, from deep underground to deep in your veins.

Light illuminates. When it is in the distance, like a lighthouse, it helps you find where you are. When it is in your hand, like a lantern, it helps you see your path. When it is in your eyes, like a floodlight, it is blinding. When you are trying to hide, it is painfully revealing. In a fireplace, it is delightful. In the attic, it is devastating.

Jesus talks about being the salt of the earth and then talks about salt losing its flavor.

I don't understand. I mean, I understand the metaphor - if salt ever were to lose its saltiness, it would be worthless. But I don't know if it ever could happen. If you search online for salt and light, you get thousands of sermons on this text. Lots of preachers explain this metaphor, but I still don't exactly understand. I just know that Jesus says that the people who live with this new routine will have a life-giving influence.

On the other hand, I think that if I heard Jesus talk about light, I'd get the point. He talks about the pointlessness of a light that is under a basket.

I do understand that. A basket over a lamp hides it. Until, of course, the basket catches on fire and burns up everything around.

With these two images of absurdities of salt and light, Jesus says, "Be what you are made to be, do what you are made to do."

In other words, routinely live following him.

5

Not good enough (Matthew 5:20)

Now the conversation turns.

Jesus was always surrounded by people who had nothing left to lose. As they learned they could trust him, he attracted "sinners" and prostitutes, tax collectors and Palestinians, wealthy women and line workers. They sat closer and closer. But almost always, standing at the edge of the crowd, keeping a safe distance from the inferior classes, were the religious authorities. The ancient version of snarky bloggers. They were the people with carefully cultivated reputations for perfection. And Jesus knew their presence was shaping the whole conversation about a new routine.

The old routine was pervasive. He needed to help people understand that something new was possible. That it was, in fact, necessary.

So let's do a little exercise that Jesus describes.

Pick the most spiritual person you know. The one who knows all the rules. The one who keeps them all. The one who has spent his whole life studying and then living out that study. The one who has cleaned every bad habit out of her closet. The one who prays every day. The one who has a quiet time every night. The one who has memorized more of the Bible than you have read. The one who, try as you might, has no faults. (I mean, really has no faults.)

Pick the person that is so good that you decide that there is no hope for you. The person that you try to argue with about God and they win every time. The one that seems to have no questions, no doubts. The one that knows the answer every time in Sunday school. The one that has just the right video to recommend for that problem, that has the right verse, that knows the right song, that sings with the right choir.

You know that person?

Jesus says that they aren't going to heaven. Neither are you. Neither am I.

Of course, he doesn't stop there. Or, more accurately, he doesn't end there.

He starts with, "unless you are far more righteous than that person…"

Those people, who were called Pharisees by the people listening to Jesus this day he was sitting on a hillside talking, were the perfect people. And when Jesus says that even they weren't righteous enough, a murmur must have wafted through the crowd. People must have looked around the edges of the crowd for a Pharisee. People must have felt a mixture of fear and despair.

Jesus had said the Pharisees didn't measure up (fear). He said no one did (despair).

Though he's not talking about it here, not yet, it's good that he was going to offer to be righteousness.

6

You have heard it said (Matthew 5:21)

And now Jesus begins to illustrate what he means by not measuring up. He's going to take what everyone had thought of as spiritually sufficient and change the routine.

He starts in a way that is very familiar to all of us who like to attack the status quo: "You have heard it said that, but I say...".

How many of us spend much of our lives based on "you have heard it said?"

"This is what *we've* been taught," we hear from our parents and our churches and our teachers. "This is how it *should* happen. This is what's been passed on from generation to generation."

I know that it is easy to pick on "this is how we've always done it." I know the story about the soldier who stands at attention elbow bent, his hand by his shoulder, for no reason other than when his predecessor's predecessor stood in that place, there was a horse's halter to hold on to.

Picking on that kind of thinking is easy.

What Jesus did is much more challenging.

In the next section of his sermon, six times he starts paragraphs with "You have heard it said." Each time the rule came from the law given to Moses. And then Jesus makes the rule more difficult. What started as rules about behavior Jesus turns into rules about *attitudes* toward behavior.

Murder, adultery, divorce, oaths, revenge, love. Jesus captures a list of topics at the core of being human, a list of topics all about relationships between human. And then he takes this list and makes it apply to every one of us.

We may not murder but we all know hatred, for example. We may not sleep around with our bodies, but we do with our eyes and our minds. We feel vindicated by vengeance, but we all fail to bend over backwards.

This sermon's list of blessings would have made many listeners feel good about themselves. The hard-driving list of reinterpreted obligations would have hammered at the audience, one blow after another. Because, after all, while I don't hate anyone, if I am honest with myself and with you, I do consider some people foolish. People I know. People who know me.

It's what I do. That's like murder.

I confess.

7

I'm sorry you are mad at me (Matthew 5:23-24)

If you are taking your sacrifice to the temple, Jesus says, and you remember that someone is angry at you, go to them and make it right. Then come back and offer your sacrifice, give your gift, fulfill your obligation. We read that and we want to start a conversation with him.

But Jesus, what if they made up the problem?

[silence]

Okay, that doesn't happen very often. But Jesus, what if they don't forgive me?

[silence]

But Jesus, what if I've tried everything I could think of and they are still angry with me?

[silence]

Okay, I will have tried. And their response isn't my problem. But Jesus, why should it matter if they are mad at me? You just talked about me being angry and that being like murder. And I'm not angry.

[silence]

But Jesus, are you saying that if I know someone is mad at me and I don't do anything to stop it, it's like letting them commit murder and not stepping in?

[silence]

But Jesus, are you saying that my knowing that someone is upset with me might interfere with my ability to bring you my gifts? That I might be worried about avoiding them as I walk around?

[silence]

But Jesus, isn't there time later? Or are you suggesting that it is more important to have relationship restored with people than it is to bring you a sacrifice?

[silence]

But Jesus, are you suggesting that if a name comes to my mind when I am bringing my gift to worship, that maybe that name is one that *you* are reminding me of, that maybe you know what is happening?

[silence]

But Jesus, what if I just don't want to? Can't it just be me and God in worship without worrying about other people?

[silence]

But Jesus, I can't. I need help.

"Okay."

8

Lust is an action (Matthew 5:27-30)

If you are the president and talk about lust in an interview in *Playboy*, and you are a Southern Baptist, you get in trouble. People laugh at you. People think you are odd. People don't want to understand you. You almost lose the election. That's what happened to Jimmy Carter.

That's what happens when you take this 'following the words of Jesus' process too seriously.

Or maybe Jimmy Carter was not taking it too seriously.

In Matthew 5:27-30, Jesus says that he isn't really interested in technical obedience, in being able to say "I looked but I didn't touch." What he understands pretty clearly is that when we are thinking about one thing, we aren't thinking about something else. When we are thinking about green, for example, we aren't thinking about blue. When we are thinking about "This Old House" we aren't thinking about "CSI: New York." When we are thinking about ice cream sundaes, we are not thinking about successfully completing marathons.

When we are thinking about that girl's body, we are not thinking about loving our wife.

In fact, when we take a second look or a third look toward *her*, we are taking a second step and a third step away from understanding more about our wife, about how to love her in the same way, with the same intensity and purity that Christ loves the church and gave himself up for her.

Adultery is violating the marriage covenant. And the violations start when you turn away, not when you touch someone else.

It's funny. I think, "How would Jesus know? Why so much intensity that he uses the image of gouging out an eye or chopping off a hand?"

I'm pretty sure he didn't really want people to do that. But maybe the answer is in the image I quoted about Christ loving the church, the one from Ephesians 5. Maybe, just maybe, Jesus understood being the rejected one in a relationship and didn't want anyone else to know that feeling.

9

But you said... (Matthew 5:33-37)

We make promises all the time. They often come in a series. Kind of like this:

- "Yes. "

- "I will do that."

- "If you ask me, then I will do that."

- "I will do that, cross my heart and hope to die."

- "If you will do this, just this one time, I promise that I will do that, I swear on a stack of Bibles."

- "I know that I've promised a thousand times and I've messed up every time, but this time, I'm really, really serious, and I mean it this time, and see, my fingers aren't crossed behind my back and this time I won't try to weasel out if it and this time, I promise on my mother's grave that I will do it."

- "You have to believe me; I am completely different this time. You can ask anyone, I swear to you, I will do this."

- "Please, what do I have to do for you to believe that I will do this?"

- "May God strike me dead if I don't do this."

When Jesus started talking about oaths and about swearing he wasn't talking about the #@%&* kind of swearing. He was talking about people who couldn't be trusted. He was talking about people who had broken their word and had to add support to their commitments. He was talking about people who had said that they would do something and hadn't and then said, "This time I will, so help me God."

He was talking about people like us.

The simplest thing to do to have people trust you is to say "yes" and then do "yes."

Of course, in the middle of a busy day when there isn't time to think clearly, it may be simple to say "yes" just to get the noise of requests to stop. But Jesus wanted "yes" to actually mean "yes."

It's about trust.

10

You caught me skipping (Matthew 5:31-32)

One of the things about following Jesus is that you can't skip what you don't like.

As a writer, I can, of course. I can jump wherever I want. I can ignore whatever I want. I can make topic choices however I want. If you are reading through Matthew while reading these words, you may have noticed that I went from murder to adultery to oaths. I skipped divorce.

It's uncomfortable, that passage. No one is in favor of murder. No one is in favor of adultery. No one cares about oaths. And really, in general, no one is in favor of divorce. But divorce is really hard for us.

What do we say, after all? We feel like we are judging family and friends if we talk about it in terms of right and wrong. And yet Jesus here puts strict parameters on divorce.

And Jesus didn't skip the subject.

In keeping with the contrasts ("You have heard it said, I say to you"), he first states the technically acceptable standard for obedience and then sets his standard.

And it is a difficult standard.

Here is what I do when someone asks me what I think about difficult texts, challenging words from Jesus. I walk around my desk, and I sit next to them; I put us on the same side of the words. I want it to be clear that the Scripture is speaking to both of us.

And I say, "Here's what it says. Let's talk about why you are wondering."

If someone is wondering what the text means because they want to judge, *that's* wrong.

If someone is wondering because they want permission to do what they know is wrong, then *that's* wrong.

But if someone is wondering because they want to understand what Jesus means, then we talk about options.

The opposite of skipping isn't Bible thumping. It's Bible listening.

11

So, what about divorce? (Matthew 5:31-32)

So I have to go back and talk about divorce. Because Jesus did.

What he said was this: the law, as recorded by Moses, allowed men to break their promise about marriage because people would do it anyway. By giving your wife a note of dismissal, she was gone, no particular reason given.

And then what Jesus said is that if you break your promise like this, if you break a covenant on a whim, if you just decide that you are the most important being in the universe, what you are actually saying is that your wife was sleeping around. And anyone who marries her gets caught in the sequence.

This would have been a particularly intimate image for Jesus. Throughout the law and the prophets, God had been using marriage as a metaphor for his relationship with people. No matter how much the people wandered, no matter how much the wife gave reason for dismissal, God never did. And Jesus was sitting on that rock, talking to that crowd, looking into the faces of people who would abandon him and deny him and ask for his death and telling husbands that they needed to stay committed.

I understand we can identify all kinds of reasons for people to break promises. I understand that there is pain and abuse and abandonment. I understand that this passage is used to add to that abuse.

But what if we start from the other end of reasoning? What if we look at why God wants the promise to be kept? And we do everything in our power not to look at the boundaries to see how far we can go but to commit. To routinely look at the steps of the one who showed how far he would go to love.

12

Someone in your life is going to go too far (Matthew 5:38-42)

Someone, this week, is going to go too far.

Someone is going to ask more of you than they should ask.

Someone is going to insult you.

Someone is going to ask for more than they deserve.

Someone is going to go too far.

You know that it will happen.

You are going to have to decide, in that moment, how to react.

It will be completely understandable to snap back. It will make complete sense to do precisely what is required and no more. It is to be expected to do what is expected.

I wouldn't hold it against you at all, as long as you will give me the room. It is an acceptable part of our routine.

But then, of course, we both would have to figure out what Jesus meant when he said to do the unexpected, to go beyond the acceptable response to the insults and attacks sure to come this week.

Jesus is saying to plan to respond differently, well in advance of the insult.

He says you are going to get the back of the hand. Someone will insult you with a slap to the face. You have been trained and permitted and encouraged to slap that person back. Your tongue is ready to return the criticism; your mind is rehearsing the devastatingly sarcastic reply.

Jesus says, don't do it. Instead, start planning now, start rehearsing in your head, turning your face and silently offering the other cheek.

"Wait," you say.

Does that mean that if it is an abusive situation that we are to stay in it?

"Wait," I say, "*are* you in an abusive situation?"

If you are, call me. Let's get you out. But if you aren't and you are raising that question rather than preparing for how you will respond to the insult that will come this week, prepare.

Be like God (Matthew 5:43-48)

"Be like God. Love your enemies."

That's what Jesus is saying in Matthew 5:43-48.

It sounds like an impossible standard.

Jesus starts by talking about God's treatment of enemies.

In an arid country, rain is life. And when it rains, it rains on everyone. Though we wish there were little clouds that followed some people and little suns that followed others, it rains on everyone.

"It's not fair," we say when good stuff happens to people we don't like, to people who are unkind. "It's not fair," we say when bad stuff happens to people we like, to people who are caring and loving and spiritual.

But God is capable of being even-handed, of giving the warm and cool, the sun and the rain, on farmers who love him and on farmers who despise him. He is capable of being even-handed, of letting roses grow in the gardens of people who plot destruction and in the gardens of the godly.

And it isn't fair at all.

But it gives credence to the command to love your enemies. Because God does.

But what if they are actually persecuting you? What then? How do you love them then?

Jesus says, "Pray for them." And though we would tend to have those prayers sound like "God, destroy them," that's not much of an option, at least not from Jesus.

Part of following Jesus is to look at how he lived and to live like that. And when we look at Luke 23, and we read that Jesus said, "Father, forgive them, because they don't know what they are doing," we find out what he meant by saying, "pray for your persecutors."

Hanging on a cross, praying for his enemies, asking for forgiveness.

Like Father, like Son.

14

Like the hypocrites do (Matthew 6:1-18)

"The church is full of hypocrites."

That's what people say. I've heard it said. It's hard to argue with that statement, mostly because I look in the mirror. I go to church. I have huge gaps between what I do and what I want to do. I say noble things and don't do them. That's usually what people are talking about when they talk about hypocrites and church.

"You say you're a Christian and then you do that?"

But in Matthew 6, Jesus seems to be thinking about a different kind of hypocrite, people who **do** noble things but for the wrong reasons. He identifies three areas of behavior where hypocrites do things the wrong way, behaviors perfect for creating an appearance of spirituality: giving, praying, and fasting. Helping out poor people, that's important to do. And praying, what could be more spiritual than praying? And fasting, well, that kind of self-denial is amazing.

But, Jesus says, don't be public, be private.

Don't pray to attract attention. Don't fast for the compliments you get, for the good feeling you have when people notice your actions. And don't give in a way that makes it easy for people to notice your actions.

If the only time you give is when you get a tax deduction or when you find out someone else is giving or when there is a wall of recognition, then by all means help. But don't expect God to care. If the only time you talk with God is when people are listening, and then with a deep voice and flowery language, enjoy their comments about how much they enjoy when you pray. But don't expect God to care what you say.

Why *should* he care? Think about it. You wouldn't care. You wouldn't listen to what I said if I talked to you only when people were listening.

That said, God is very interested in giving, praying and fasting. As Jesus talks, he contrasts recognition from people with recognition from God. He suggests that the latter is more important than the former.

I've heard people wonder after reading this passage whether God would suddenly ignore them if someone found out about their giving. I know of people who are concerned about praying in public, who are afraid of praying so other people hear because of their fear of pride. But that's because we focus on the 'don't' part of these sentences and the potential of punishment. What if Jesus isn't talking about avoiding pride? What if Jesus' greatest concern isn't with avoiding people knowing. *What if his biggest interest is encouraging a conspiratorial relationship with the Father?*

You know the feeling when you work with someone else to plan a wonderful surprise? A surprise where some third person will get what they've always wanted? A surprise where that third person must never know how this happened, but that's okay because you and your co-conspirator can celebrate together?

That's what Jesus is inviting, that kind of relationship with the Father. A routine of working together.

Work with the Father in your giving. The people you are helping? Do your best to not let them know. Do your best to not let the press know, to not brag about it, even quietly to a few close friends. In fact, Jesus says, don't even let your hands talk to each other. But know that the Father knows. Know that you can share a laugh, a knowing wink, with Him.

15

"I love to hear you pray" (Matthew 6:5-6)

I confess. I have been told that I pray well in public.

I don't quite know what do to with that compliment. I mean, on one hand I'm not talking to the person complimenting me. I'm talking to God. It is *almost* completely irrelevant whether she loves to hear me pray. What matters far more is whether *God* loves to hear me pray. In fact, there have been times that people have expressed concern that I pray too quietly or that my voice gets softer. I want to say to them, "I'm not talking to you."

On the other hand, I have times when I am responsible for praying so that people *can* hear. There are times that I am leading in prayer, helping other people to focus on conversing with God. At those times, I'm like a spokesperson for a large group. One person talks, the others nod and agree and say, "Yes, that's how we feel, that's what we think, too."

There are other times when I am praying for (in place of) someone else. They are so consumed with whatever is happening in their lives that they cannot give voice to what they are feeling, to the depth of their pain. Or they cannot think clearly. In those moments, I am praying aloud so that they can share in my words.

I give these examples to help us think through what Jesus was saying when he told those listening to not pray on street corners and out in public, but to go home, go into a room, and shut the door. Does this mean that God only hears when no one else can?

Clearly not. There are prayers of Jesus and his followers recorded, which means someone heard. So here's the core question: Are we praying for compliments? Or for communion? Are we routinely talking with God regardless of who else is around?

16

So why do we have to ask? (Matthew 6:7-8)

Sometimes I know exactly what our children Andrew and Hope need. I can look ahead and know that they will be in *that* situation and will need *that* solution.

I know it. But I may not tell them. I may wait for them to ask.

Sometimes they decide to ask for help ahead of time. And Nancy and I can take care of their need.

Sometimes they come to me at the last minute. Maybe I can help; maybe I can't.

Sometimes they come to me afterwards and say, "I should have asked."

Let's think about my actions.

Why do I let them suffer? Do you think I'm a bad parent for not acting even if I'm not asked? Do you think that I should anticipate their every difficulty and prevent it? If they forget their homework assignment, should I always take it to school? Do you think that they will learn about taking responsibility or will they merely take me for granted?

Is it possible that sometimes I might know what is going on and choose to wait for them to ask for help?

Is it possible that sometimes they ask for help and set in process the things that will help them and because they don't see what they expect, they keep begging me to do something?

Is it possible that they spend enormous amounts of energy worrying about what I am already taking care of?

Is it possible that my action for their good will happen on my timetable rather than theirs?

Is it possible that what they call "not caring" and what they call "ignoring" and what they call "not listening" and what they call "forever" are none of those things?

And if it is possible that in my wisdom as a dad, I act differently than our children expect but still for their good, isn't it possible God does, too?

The Lord's Prayer: a preface (Matthew 6:9-13)

After talking about praying, Jesus gives his followers a model prayer. It's not that every time we pray this is all we should say. There are several times that Jesus is talking to his Father, and he doesn't say these words at all. There are prayers all the way through Paul's letters, and he never says these words.

On the other hand, Jesus does say "Here's how you should pray." So it's worth spending some time reflecting on what Jesus was telling us to do.

17

Lord's Prayer: Our Father in heaven (Matthew 6:9)

For some people, the beginning of this prayer has to be rough.

To start with "Our Father" brings horrible memories. And the thought, "if God is like that, then I'm not interested."

As I think about this beginning, however, I realize that Jesus knew.

Jesus knew that some men would be hopelessly cruel to their daughters. He knew that some families would shatter through the selfishness of one or the other or both. He knew that the image of father would be a challenge for many dads. (I think about it sometimes. I realize that the image our kids have of God as father is shaped by their image of Jon as father, and I am chagrined.)

And so Jesus, in his knowledge of what families were going to be like, good and ill, starts this model of prayer by focusing on the closest, dearest, strongest, healthiest, most life-giving, most protection-offering person he knew. His Father in heaven.

Before any requests are made. Before any apologies are offered. Before any transactions are begun, relationship is established. This is to be a familial relationship, a perfect, paternal relationship. Everything you ever wished for a dad to be is being offered at the beginning of this prayer, this conversation.

If we have questions about starting the conversation with relationship, later Jesus uses a story to show what the relationship is like (Luke 15:19).

He described a son who left home and messed up and shamed the family. The son comes back and, as Jesus tells it says, "'Father I have sinned against heaven and against you. I am no longer worthy to be called your son.' But the father...'"

"But the father." This father has run to the son. The father has waited for years for this conversation to start. Jesus says the father won't even let the son finish the speech. This is a father who knew exactly what the son had done and wouldn't let him finish the speech. He called for servants to bring new clothes and start party preparations.

So when Jesus says to start with "our *Father*," Jesus knows the party that's about to happen.

Lord's Prayer: We pray that your name will always be kept holy (6:9)

Sometimes, when I read the Bible, I don't know what it means. So I ask. Like this:

***

Father, I realize that I don't know exactly what hallowed means.

And so for all the years I've been praying this prayer, I'm not sure I understand, exactly. Does it mean that you want me to ask *you* to keep your name special and set apart? Does it mean that you want me to affirm that your name is special, to affirm that I don't take lightly the fact that I get to call you Father?

Because I want to affirm that, I really do. But I've got to confess: sometimes I take for granted that I'm actually talking to *You*. I mean, I just starting talking as if you aren't *God*.

It's not that you don't want relationship. It's not that you don't invite me to a conversational relationship. It's more that I start talking as if you couldn't do anything about what is going on. Complaining without remembering that I'm not talking to the complaint department, I'm talking to the owner directly. Venting to a friend who has also suffered without remembering that you are the friend with really big muscles. Whining without asking. Asking without believing. Believing without doing. Doing instead of trusting.

There are always shades of not remembering that you are holy, pure, not confined to my motives. And yet, you aren't waiting to trap me in my misstatements, you are wanting to help me remember.

David almost always got this right. In his prayers he would complain or lament or identify the problem, but he would always come back to acknowledging you.

"How long will you forget me, Lord" at the beginning of Psalm 13 by the end becomes "Then I will sing to the Lord because he was so good to me."

So help me remember who you are and why that can encourage me.

Amen.

19

Lord's Prayer: Your kingdom (Matthew 6:10)

There are many debates about what the kingdom of heaven means in Matthew, about when it starts, about what Jesus means when he says "Repent because the Kingdom is at hand."

I wonder why we wonder so much? Why do we care so much about having exactly the right interpretation? Is it because we want to be kings of understanding "your kingdom"? Is it because being right will make us special?

***

Jesus, did you know how much we love to be the most right one, the most understanding one, the most humble one? Of course you knew. Otherwise, you wouldn't have made surrender so high on the list of things to talk to our Father about.

"We pray that your kingdom will come–that what you want will be done here on earth, the same as in heaven."

That's how you told us to pray about kingdom.

***

Here's why I think that he told us to pray that way, and told us to say "we pray" rather than "I pray." He wanted us to routinely be in clusters when we said these words, in community. Like a group of eight or nine people in a living room. And he wanted us to have to talk about God's kingdom coming with people who know how much we want our kingdom, or even my kingdom.

I can get pretty confident about my understanding. I can stake out what I think. And then when eight people who know me well are hearing me talk about wanting God's kingdom, there is an instant credibility check.

And when we together are asking that the Father's desire happen here as well as in heaven, we have to look each other in the eye and say, "That means in us, between us, among us, within us."

Not my kingdom. Not our kingdom. *Your kingdom.*

I guess that's pretty clear.

Lord's Prayer: Enough for today (Matthew 6:11)

Sometimes context doesn't seem to matter. Things seem clear at face value.

Like a request for bread. What could be more simple? "Give me food today. (Please)."

For the people hearing this model prayer from Jesus for the first time, the request was only partly about the future or about today. It had everything to do with the past.

Israel was in the desert, having left Egypt (with God's assistance). They were, they thought, without food (though they did have flocks of animals with them.)

They fussed about being without food. And God gave them manna. It was some kind of seed or flake or something that could be ground and made into bread. It showed up every day. Well, every day but one every week.

On that day, on the Sabbath day, they didn't get any manna. But on the day before, there was enough for two days.

Six days out of seven for forty years. It was an incredible number of "every days". It was an incredible amount of daily bread.

For Israel, wandering in the desert, the prayer that Jesus taught reflected their experience. Every day, each day, the bread for that day and no more. You had to go collect it, but you couldn't save it.

Every morning there was faith. Every morning there was food.

LORD'S PRAYER: ENOUGH FOR TODAY (MATTHEW 6:11)   41

I wonder if the daily asking was a way to remember complete dependence. I mean, *we* aren't exactly in the desert. We aren't exactly in need of daily provision. We have plenty of everything. We could almost ask for bread every two weeks, just as a way to acknowledge, on payday, that we are working hard to earn our daily bread.

For Israel, in the desert, it wasn't about their great jobs, their hard work. It was about a faithful God daily giving bread.

(To read the story of manna, see Exodus 16.)

21

Lord's Prayer: That is really hard (Matthew 6:11)

Jesus says that we are to ask God to forgive our debts as we forgive our debtors.

Jesus says that there is a correlation between our asking God for forgiveness and us forgiving other people. We are to ask for forgiveness and, it seems, tell God to forgive us in the same way *as* we forgive others.

I once heard someone say that we expect people to respond the way we would respond in the same situation. We use our motives to assess their motives. Thus, people who cheat assume that everyone would cheat. People who don't take anything seriously assume that everyone is that flexible.

People who choose to hold back forgiveness will assume that God is that way, too.

"I forgive them, but I'm watching closely for them to mess up again."

"I forgive them, but I'm keeping track."

Notice a very careful word choice.

Choose.

Many people struggle to forgive people who have intentionally hurt them deeply. "I'm trying to forgive, but it's hard," they say. And then they worry about this passage. They worry that unless they forgive, they will be punished. But they don't know how to forgive.

It's for us that this prayer exists.

Though he links the two conditionally, Jesus first allows us to ask for forgiveness. As we remember his forgiveness, forgiving becomes easier. Not easy, but possible.

Lord's Prayer: Please take care of me (Matthew 6:12-13)

"**Y**ou aren't going to leave me, are you?"

When you are getting to know someone too good to be true, you have questions. You acknowledge their greatness. You ask them for help. You acknowledge your weakness.

As you are starting to relax a bit, you are suddenly seized with fear. What if they aren't going to stick around? What if they aren't going to follow through? What if they are going to be like everyone else we have ever known in our lives, people who sometime, someday, don't come through?

We get so used to people who don't keep their word, who let us down. We are familiar with the feeling of betrayal, of abandonment, of disappointment. We watch every leader we know prove to be human, at best.

And so, having made all our requests known, we stop and we say

"Don't lead us into temptation."

"Do deliver us from evil."

"God, please don't bring us this far and leave us. Don't bring us through the week and into the weekend and then leave us alone, facing temptation. Don't do to us what you did to your own son."

There it is.

We want to be able to trust God, but we somehow can't. We look at what happens to people who follow him, who even *are* Him, and what we see undermines what we think should happen.

Jesus was led into the desert to be tempted by the devil. By the Spirit. Just two chapters ago. Jesus survived the direct testing. Now he says, "Ask the Father not to do the first part with you, and to just do the second part."

Maybe we don't have to understand the theology to say these words. Maybe we just have to give voice to our fears.

23

Fasting (Matthew 6:16-18)

Don't you love the difference choosing one word can make? One word makes things optional. One word makes them expected. One word makes you think about the perhaps. One word makes you think about the procedure. One word is about whether. One word is about how. One word is "if". One word is "when".

Jesus talks about fasting in Matthew 6:16-18. He starts this section of his sermon with "When you fast." He could have made fasting completely optional by saying "if". He could have removed fasting from consideration by not talking about it at all (thereby leaving the conversation about fasting up to commentators: "The fact that Jesus didn't mention fasting suggests that he found it an unimportant element of spiritual life.")

Instead, fasting shows up three times in Matthew's account of Jesus' life. The first time is when Jesus himself fasts for 40 days prior to his temptation. The third time is in where John's disciples ask Jesus why both they and the Pharisees fast and Jesus' disciples don't. The second time is here where Jesus is talking about how to fast.

Because Matthew is kind of a handbook for what it means to be a follower of Jesus, let's take a look at these three. One tells us that Jesus himself saw value in fasting, particularly before the beginning of his ministry. The third tells us that both groups of super-religious people saw fasting itself as an observable measure of spirituality. In the second Jesus says that if fasting is done for how it looks, then what humans think of you is all it is good for.

Said differently, if you want people to be impressed, then be public about your fasting. If you want God to listen, be incredibly private. And somehow, make fasting part of your new routine.

***

Fasting isn't supposed to be fun. It's supposed to be difficult. It's supposed to be challenging. Intentionally refraining from something that is important to you, which is essential to your well-being, is a difficult thing.

The longer the fast, the harder it is supposed to be. Spending forty days fasting, as Jesus did, has to be grueling. Spending three weeks fasting like Daniel did would be challenging. Spending a day without food for many of us triggers headaches. And with all of that difficulty, Jesus says that when we fast, people shouldn't be able to tell by looking at us.

In that comment, Jesus makes it clear that he knows people inside and out. When most of us are doing something difficult, we like other people to know. When we spent the night not sleeping, we make sure that people understand why we are cranky. We help them to have the appropriate amount of sympathy for us. We often remind people of how busy we are. We frequently help people know our burdens.

And Jesus says, when you are giving up food (or whatever you are fasting from), don't look miserable. (One translation says that the hypocrites "disfigure their faces," an apt description of us when we are trying to look like we are feeling miserable.) Instead, wash your face, comb your hair, look as alert, as happy, as normal as you can.

Will our family know that we are missing a meal? Yes, of course. Will that negate the value? Probably not. Unless we are fasting to impress them.

The hardest part of fasting may be that people won't know. Which is, of course, the point.

***

Okay. Here's the deal. I *want* to talk about fasting.

I want to talk about what the reward is.

I want to talk about this incredibly cool image that God paints in Isaiah 58 about fasting not being about being selfish and simply not eating the food you have, but about sharing a meal with people who don't have food. I would love to consider the irony that a person fasting might actually eat. Isaiah talks not about giving up food, but giving up reputation to be eating with the people that no one else will eat with.

It's not, according to God, about lying around feeling weak, but it's about actively breaking bonds, taking the time that you would spend on eating and researching injustice or breaking up fights or writing letters to the local foodbank.

It's not about reveling in my ability to choose to not eat, but it's about helping people who don't have the freedom to decide anything about anything, the people who are trapped in all kinds of bondage.

I would love to talk about the fact that the people who pursue active fasting are told by God that they can call out to him, and he will listen to them. He will hear *them* and will choose to *not* listen to the people who are involved in showy fasting, the kind that gets attention for the suffering that it inflicts on the faster.

I would love to examine things we can fast from other than food, what ways we could pursue justice. I would love to spend time working through all these things.

But I keep needing to look at my email in the odd chance that something will show up. And I keep checking my twitter feed to see if someone responded. And there are so many things I have to do, things that I cannot give up. For anything.

24

Relationship rewards (Matthew 6:20)

"*Store up treasure in heaven.*"

That's what Jesus tells us. Don't spend your energy on stuff that gets eaten up by financial declines so that you panic about how much less you are worth this week than last week. If the measure of your worth is your portfolio and the value of your portfolio declines precipitously, then your heart will decline precipitously as well.

Isn't it intriguing that this image Jesus paints of wealth being devoured rings so true in an economic decline? And isn't it intriguing how much energy the people in the mirror are putting into thinking about how many more years we are going to have to work before retirement? Isn't it intriguing how cranky and insecure and strategic we are getting?

What does it mean to store up treasure in heaven and how does that help now?

If treasures are like rewards, then the first half of Matthew 6 answers that question. Giving, praying, and fasting, done in secret, bring rewards.

What?

You mean that if I look for people in need and help them, that is storing up treasure? But how could that have reward?

You mean that if I am talking with God, that is storing up treasure? But it's conversation! It is its own reward.

You mean that if I am fasting with a smile on my face, combating injustice, bringing freedom to trapped people, that stores up treasure? But it is so fulfilling!

All three of these things that Jesus says are rewarding are rooted in deepening our relationship with God.

I've thought of storing up treasure as acquisition. But gold in heaven is the least valuable thing. The conversational relationship is the real treasure.

And treasure storage doesn't wait until heaven, it starts right now. With routine deposits.

25

Birds and flowers (Matthew 6:25-34)

The daffodils are growing in front of our house. In a month they will be bright yellow. Except for the ones that are white. Except for the ones that are pastel yellow. There will be more than last year. **We** didn't plant the extra ones.

The finches will be back soon. They will be joining the robins. They will be followed by the hummingbirds. We will feed them. But we can take no credit for them.

When people think of birds and flowers and Jesus, the ornery among us think about how they die, how some of them starve in the winter, how the flowers are often not vivid. We listen to Jesus talking about taking care of flowers and birds, about food and clothing, and we think that he falls short.

I don't think Jesus was talking about botany or ornithology. He was talking about attention.

What do we invest your attention in?

Jesus suggests some things to not invest it in. Don't invest it in worry. Don't invest it in wondering *whether* God knows (He does know). Don't invest it in what you have already asked God for (This teaching comes right after having asked God for our daily bread. Having asked for that, Jesus says, don't worry about how the Father will do it).

What do we pay attention to? *What **God** is doing.*

Jesus says to routinely seek the Kingdom as the first priority. To listen for and look for the way of living that is found there. Be part of what will last forever and get dressed in the righteous clothes. And then, Jesus says, the rest will follow. The food and drink and clothing that are needed.

Here's the new routine: Ask God what part of his Kingdom he wants you to seek right now. And seek it. And ask. And seek. And ask. And seek.

Today has enough trouble (Matthew 6:34)

I have no clue what will happen today.

I just wanted you to know that.

I spent part of one Sunday afternoon at a funeral for a woman who had been married for 65 years, who had Alzheimer's. The pastor started his message with "None of us planned to be here today."

What was interesting for this funeral is that this woman--after her family was told it would be a "matter of hours" -- lived for several days. The family had *been* planning on a funeral and couldn't even count on that happening.

I don't mean to be disrespectful at all.

I do, however, want to remind myself that even when we think we know what's coming, we don't. Death happens, or doesn't. Our child gets sick, or doesn't. Our stock crashes, or doesn't.

If we spend all of our time worrying about what might happen or planning as if nothing will happen, we will find that we have wasted a lot of energy that could have been spent on something else. Like listening to the person talking to us right now. Like asking for wisdom for the project that is happening right now. Like not procrastinating on writing that tough email because of our fear of what might happen.

Jesus said, "Seek the kingdom." In the next breath he says, "Don't worry about tomorrow."

Today has its own trouble. Today has its own opportunity to watch God work. Today we can ask God to let us be part of his work and his kingdom and his caring and his compassion and his solutions and his hope.

Interestingly, the trusting and following and obeying that we do today may well eliminate whatever it was that we were worrying might happen tomorrow.

So when you read this, whenever it is, as often as you thing about it, do this:

Say "God, let me see you today."

27

The window or the mirror (Matthew 7:1-2)

I started to write about judging but want to write without being judgmental.

I sit here creating examples of extreme finickiness and then think, "But isn't that being judgmental, reflecting my own bias against finickiness?"

And I am convicted. And I save the draft and start over.

Why? Because Jesus says the standard that I use to critique you is the one that will be used by God to examine me.

I'm tempted to be incredibly flexible in hopes that God will be accepting of me. "If I don't criticize laziness, he'll accept my laziness." "If I don't criticize anger, he'll let me be angry." Unfortunately, that approach is backwards. It assumes that I can somehow trick God.

The better approach is to start the judging with me. "God tells me not to be angry." "God tells me to be loving." "God tells me to be gentle."

There is a place for identifying injustice, for proclaiming freedom for captives. That process, mentioned often, involves making judgments about acceptable and unacceptable behavior. But the starting place for such judgments is always in the mirror, rather than in the window.

Before I talk about your lies, for example, have I been honest with God and myself about my motives for pointing out your lies, about my actions in lying to my professor that I had read the religious ethics book that I hadn't read, about my unwillingness to be honest about why work isn't getting done, about the wedding ceremony income that I didn't bother to report to the IRS in 2004, about the amount of time that it really takes to do projects?

Have I been honest with God?

Then, having been honest with God, will I be likely to judge or be more likely to invite you to freedom?

28

A sense of humor (Matthew 7)

We are too serious.

Okay, so maybe some of us laugh sometimes. And some of us laugh all the time. And some of us frown most of the time. But most of the time most people have some amount of laughter.

Until we pick up the Bible, that is. Then we get serious. Too serious. We look at words and sentences and paragraphs as we do everything we can to find all the meaning we can. We want to get it right. And in the process of serious analysis, we miss the fun stuff. And there is fun stuff.

This whole chapter, full of sticks in the eyes and hogs and dogs and houses built on sand and rock, paints vivid images of Kingdom living. Jesus wants his audience, including us, to have a clear picture of what he's saying.

For example, Jesus wants to help an audience understand the problem in judging. He wants to help them make no mistake about how silly it is to try to be God, to try to be the one who decides who is right and who is wrong. So he creates a picture, one that he would know well (being a carpenter and all).

Imagine a guy in the shop. He's working along and ends up with a piece of sawdust in his eye. It hurts. It's a hassle. He asks his buddy for help. Up to this point, the buddy has been bent over, as if he's looking for something. And now he turns, and we clearly see the baseball bat in his eye. Now, it's not a bat, it's a branch. No wait, it's a log. There is a log in the other guy's eye.

And as the second guy approaches the first guy (in their mind's eye), people start laughing. It's more like the Three Stooges than a sermon. This is completely ridiculous. Everyone is laughing at the image of a man trying to look around a bat to see sawdust.

And then Jesus says "Hypocrites."

And suddenly, we all get it.

29

On hogs and dogs (Matthew 7:6)

As much as we work to understand and explain what Jesus said, we need to be honest: sometimes he wasn't clear.

At times his obfuscation, his ambiguity was purposeful. He even says that he is speaking obscurely at times. However, in the middle of a fairly clear sermon, when he seems to be trying to be clear, he says this:

"Do not give dogs what is sacred; do not throw your pearls to pigs. If you do, they may trample them under their feet, and then turn and tear you to pieces."

We read it and say, "What?!"

He just talked about not judging. He just talked about taking the baseball bat out of your own eye before worrying about the splinter in someone else's eye. And then he calls people dogs and hogs.

That seems pretty judgmental to me.

I'm pretty sure that the argument, "Jesus can say that because he knows people" doesn't apply. He's telling *us* to identify them.

What is likely, according to commentators, is that Jesus is offering a cautionary note to his judgment words. While we are not to be quick to judge, we have to acknowledge that some people are intentionally destructive. They choose to wreck good stuff, to destroy, to bully, to trample.

Be careful, he says, what you give to destructive people.

But what does that mean? Does it mean not to give too much time to people who are more interested in consuming that conversing? Does it mean don't give leadership to those who will use it to wreck? Does it mean not to give clear explanations of the gospel to those who use it to destroy?

For me, one day, it meant telling a man named Harold to leave the church grounds. He was trampling people.

No questions asked.

Waiting is hard (Matthew 7:7-12)

We all have stories about God not answering our prayer. We asked for help on the test. We failed. We asked for healing for the child. She died. We asked "Why?" We didn't hear anything.

Given our experience, many of us read these words that Jesus said and we cringe:

"Ask and it will be given to you; seek and you will find; knock and the door will be opened to you. For everyone who asks receives; he who seeks finds; and to him who knocks, the door will be opened. (Matthew 7:7-8)

And so we learn to use qualifiers. Or we don't pray at all. But what if Jesus actually was telling the truth? What if "everyone" really means "every one?" What if every time we ask we receive an answer, but we aren't listening?

Let's try this image:

A two-year-old is riding in a stroller through a store asking for that. And that. And that. If the parent keeps moving past all of the items, we may get upset.

Except the store isn't Toys'R'Us, it's Lowe's. And the aisle isn't toys, it's pesticides. And the quiet parent already told the child that they were fixing the sandbox.

With focus, the parent gets to the bags of sand. Which are not at all exciting to a two-year-old. The journey through the rest of the story is loud and the ride home is sleepy, after the tears subside. After a nap, during which the sand goes into the box, the child is taken outside and placed in the sand, where the parent also sits.

The requests of a two-year-old for what would kill are often refused.
The requests of a two-year-old for what gives life are often granted.
But two-year olds can't read the labels, and don't know the plans.
They must trust.

**

"But I'm not a two-year-old," we say. "And besides, comparing people to God isn't appropriate anyway."

Really? Are you sure?

Because that's exactly what Jesus does to help us understand how God listens to us.

He's talking to the crowd on the hillside. He's been talking to everyone, but now he speaks directly to the guys.

"How many of you, when your kid asks you to pass the bread, would hand him a stone?"

Immediately, some of us imagine teasing our kids that way. We can see ourselves at a picnic, tossing a tennis ball instead of a roll. But then we think about when our child is actually hungry, actually in need of food. We move away from teasing then. We get serious. We pass the bread.

"Or if he asks for a fish, would you really hand him a snake?"

Not a plastic snake, not a tease. A real snake, something deadly rather than life-giving. When we hear about parents who do this, we are horrified. We can't imagine.

"If you, being evil, do good things for your kids, how much more will your heavenly Father…"

Faces light up all across the hillside. "You mean, this fierce love I have for my children, this sense of protection, this desire for their good, this willingness to scold to save them, this willingness to absorb pain so they only feel some, this celebration of what they can do well, this encouragement in difficulty, all of what I feel for my children, that's how God loves me?"

Yes.

Jesus knew the fierce love His Father and his stepfather had for him. He knew one could illustrate the other.

Even today.

31

Wanna do something about it? (Matthew 7:12)

All the rules. All the warnings. All the cautionary tales. All the words. Everything that his audience had been learning since birth, Jesus said, could be summed up in one phrase. We call it the golden rule. We make it a wall plaque. We teach it to little children to train them to share.

"So in everything, do to others what you would have them do to you, for this sums up the Law and the Prophets." (Matthew 7:12)

This is a summary sentence, not just of the Law and the Prophets, but of everything Jesus has been saying for the past three chapters.

You really don't want people to hate you, right? (murder). You really don't want people to pick out one thing about you and desire that thing rather than you, do you? (lust). You really don't want people taking your clothing or making you serve them.

What you want is to be loved. What you want is to be respected. What you want is be a person, to matter. And when we don't want those things, it is often because they have been, one way or another, beaten from our souls.

And, Jesus says, "That standard? Use it."

But there is something missing from this sentence. We think that it needs a little incentive clause: "and they will treat you the same". Because we want to know that if we respect, we'll be respected. If we love, we will be loved. If we listen, we will be listened to.

That clause isn't here. Because Jesus doesn't make any claims about what *they* will do if we do this. He doesn't offer any manipulation principles. He just invites obedience.

Gates (Matthew 7:13-14)

I have written elsewhere about deliberate practice. Simply, it is choosing to work in a focused way on the weakest parts of what you are best at. Such specific work can, I think, apply in following Jesus.

It came to mind when looking at what Jesus said about gates and roads.

"Enter through the narrow gate. For wide is the gate and broad is the road that leads to destruction, and many enter through it. But small is the gate and narrow the road that leads to life, and only a few find it." [Matthew 7:13-14]

Lots of people talk about following, but not many follow through. Many of us talk about what we ought to do, but few people actually do those things. Many people lay their hand on the latch, but few lift it.

I'm pretty sure that Jesus isn't talking about artificially narrowed gates, those with narrowly defined boundaries of human rules that count. He doesn't need to. He has already clearly identified edges that talk about hate and lust and lies and religious ostentation and praying only for an audience and ungraceful judging. Those edges make the gate pretty narrow.

And yet, those edges make for a sense of hope. Treating people that lovingly, loving God that simply, bring a sense of clarity. We can't measure up without asking for help. Jesus is available to help. To enter the gate, to walk that path, we have to give up our ability to try to live successfully with unmeetable standards, but in the giving up, living becomes relationship.

It takes routine deliberate choices. Choosing to follow, choosing to focus, choosing to refine that part today, this part tomorrow.

But choosing isn't easy. It's easier to just do it all. Jesus seems to suggest that's destruction.

33

Aftermath (Matthew 7:15-23)

Some people look spiritual for all the wrong reasons. Jesus singles them out. He calls them "false prophets."

Why do they choose to be false? Because some people trust spiritual-looking people for all the wrong reasons.

Jesus offers a couple warnings near the end of his lesson.

People can look like good people *because* they are bad people. My guess is that they are very good at the externals of looking like sheep. Their credentials are perfect. The costume fits well. They are better at being sheep than most sheep. But inside they aren't just bad sheep. They are wolves.

Don't look at what teachers say, Jesus says, look at the results of what they say. Shifting metaphors, he suggests that any tree can glue the right kind of leaves on, but only apple trees can naturally grow apples. He will take this image further in John 15 where he talks about us being branches attached to his vine. The fruit will be Jesus' fruit.

I struggle with this fruit-bearing requirement. I wonder, often, whether my writing invites people to say "good thought" or "that hurts" instead of helping them change from the inside. I know that both compliments and change *can* happen. I want always to be aware of helping people take the next step, to think about the next lesson, to ask Jesus the next question.

It's interesting how concerned Jesus is with actions, with behavior, with obedience. Here he says,

"Not everyone who says to me, 'Lord, Lord,' will enter the kingdom of heaven, but only he who does the will of my Father who is in heaven."

And he will reinforce this message at the end of the book of Matthew (28:20):

"Teach them to obey everything I have commanded."

To implement this idea of looking for results, look at what follows behind teachers and preachers and each other and yourself. Are there baskets of fruit or sheep carcasses?

Just one thing (Matthew 7:24)

Many people heard many things in church last Sunday. Many words, many challenges, many opportunities. Many invitations, many explanations, many ideas.

All of the things we heard can confuse our ability to obey. Every discussion is an opportunity for confusion as well as clarity. All of the information can become noise.

However, today we have the opportunity to pick one thing and do it.

Just one. Out of all the messages, just one.

It's not that they don't all have value. It's that Jesus talked about how to build, and as I understand the process of building, I think it starts with doing one thing at a time.

Jesus says,

"Therefore everyone who hears these words of mine and puts them into practice is like a wise man who built his house on the rock" (Matthew 7:24).

A builder adds only one board at a time, one brick at a time. A builder fastens each piece to the previous piece, providing great stability. It isn't enough to build an inventory of boards, piles of brick. A full warehouse is not a finished house.

Obedience is what builds on a solid foundation. Doing what Jesus said to do. Listening and then acting. Go back to Sunday. All of the things we heard are piled in the warehouse, available, but not used. Our responsibility is to grab one board and put it in place.

Trusting was one of the things I heard the Sunday before I wrote this. Trusting was one of the things I taught. Trusting that maybe I don't have to keep all the possibilities in the air, doing none of them. Trusting that maybe, by picking one and doing it, I can learn how to obey, a skill that Jesus says is like building on a rock.

But they all look so possible.

Sandstorm (Matthew 7:24-27)

If the wise are those who build on rock, the foolish are those who build on sand.

Sand shifts. Sand moves. Sand is a million pieces of rock. Sand is all the same substance as the rock but in pieces too small to give any support. Sand is a collection of completely independent individuals. Sand is more comfortable for sleeping than rock. Sand is easier to mold into shapes, which are less durable than rock. Sand is great for playing. Sand is good for polishing things smooth. Sand is part of glass. Sand drifts.

Rock is heavy. Rock is durable. Rock doesn't get blown away. Rock takes a lot to move. Rock isn't very flexible. Rock is connected. Rock isn't very comfortable. Rock can be carved but not molded. Rock can be polished.

Sometimes we take in thousands of pieces of stuff, or we look for answers from lots of people, and we pile them up like sand. We move them around til they conform to our likes and dislikes. We add some water so that the pieces will stick and look like something solid.

Sometimes we spend a lot of time creating the appearance of obedience. We build a structure that looks the same as all the rest of the structures around. But under the surface, where no one can see, there isn't much that is solid.

Whatever sand is good for, supporting a structure isn't one of those things. Which is why Jesus used it as an example of a foolish place to build a house. The example was clear to everyone listening.

Sometimes, if we just did what Jesus told us to do, we'd be a lot more stable. But it seems harder to build something that will last. Forever.

36

Routinely: a summary

So what are the routines of the Kingdom of Heaven? Rather than talking about rules, let me suggest some behaviors Jesus talks about.

People who are following Jesus:

Routinely keep their word.

Routinely ask God for daily bread

Routinely see their poverty.

Routinely look away from people as objects and toward the people we love.

Routinely give up what is good for a bit to see what is great a little more clearly.

Routinely forgive.

Routinely ask for forgiveness.

Routinely seek the good of people who wish them ill.

Routinely go above what is expected.

Routinely ask, "Have I been honest with God?"

Routinely defer to God's priorities instead of their own.

Routinely say. "God, let me see you today."

Routinely choose against stuff and choose for God.

Routinely trust rather than routinely worry.

Routinely ask.

Routinely knock.

Routinely seek.

Routinely examine their motives.

Routinely examine their hearts.
Routinely learn more about this new routine.

Afterword

We've spent more than 14,000 words discussing what Jesus said in 2,500. That's five times as many words. And I've skimmed over many things. So go back and read what Jesus said. And then, together, let's live it. Routinely.

I don't know what to call what I write. It feels pretentious to call it a commentary. It sounds too churchy to talk about a devotional. What I tell myself is that I write "daily essays simply describing following Jesus." I do that at 300wordsaday.com. And that's where this collection started.

I am grateful to my wife Nancy and our children Andrew and Hope who have spent a lot of time in some other room while I was writing, and then have talked with me and taught me how to live. I am grateful to Becky and Rob and Rich and Joe and Cheryl and Paul, among others, who have been faithful friends and good questioners. I am grateful to a couple of small groups at Grabill Missionary Church that held me accountable to living what I teach. And I am grateful to Jesus for speaking a great sermon and then being patient with me while I tried to explain it.

If this was helpful, let someone know. If you have questions, let me know. You can email me at jon.swanson@socialmediachaplain.com.

Printed in Great Britain
by Amazon